Careers in Sports Law

Kenneth L. Shropshire, Esq.

Edited by
William D. Henslee
Sara Vlajcic

American Bar Association
Law Student Division
Standing Committee on Professional Utilization and
Career Development

Library of Congress Catalog Card Number: 90-80005
ISBN 0-89707-526-9

American Bar Association
750 North Lake Shore Drive
Chicago, Illinois 60611

2 3 4 5 6 7 8   03 02 01 00 99 98

Foreword

The American Bar Association's Career Series is designed to give students and beginning practitioners practical information on choosing and following career paths in the practice of law. Books in the series offer realistic, first-hand accounts of practicing law in specialized substantive areas and guidance on setting and reaching career goals.

The Career Series evolved during the ABA's 1982 Annual Meeting as a joint project of the Section of Economics of Law Practice, the Law Student Division, and the Standing Committee on Professional Utilization and Career Development. Working together, these three entities formed the Career Series Steering Committee which is now the ABA's official clearinghouse of career-oriented publications. The members of this committee are lawyers, law students, and administrators themselves and understand the need for educated career choices. They have geared the Career Series toward meeting the needs of students and lawyers contemplating career decisions.

Since 1982 many committee members have worked to produce this series of books, and we would like to thank some of them. Gary Munneke, Theodore Orenstein, Monica Bay, Julie Moore, Joseph Cassachi, Thomas Wynn, Lynn Strudler, Carol Kanarek, Ellen Wayne, Peggy Podell and Percy Luney have all been instrumental in establishing, developing, and maintaining the Career Series. In addition, the committee has relied on ABA staff, including Hope Bulger, Kathryn Wiley, Joe Weintraub, Paula Tsurutani, and Jane Johnston.

Our committee's goal is to help lawyers secure satisfying jobs in their chosen areas of practice. To this end, the Career Series Steering Committee presents this publication to complement the Career Series.

William D. Henslee
Chairman, American Bar Association
Career Series Steering Committee

Dedication and Acknowledgment

To my family, with special thanks to my wife, Diane, for enduring this and several other projects. I would also like to acknowledge the invaluable research assistance of Stefanie C. Reichel, and thank Percy R. Luney, Jr., Ellen Wayne, Peggy L. Podell, Lynn Stephens Strudler, and Barbara J. Lano for reviewing the manuscript.

About the Author

Kenneth L. Shropshire is an Assistant Professor of Legal Studies at the Wharton School of the University of Pennsylvania. He also practices as a legal and business consultant to individuals and organizations in the sports and entertainment industries.

Mr. Shropshire received an A.B. in economics from Stanford University and a J.D. from Columbia Law School. He has written several articles on issues involving professional and amateur sports and has a book forthcoming from the University of Pennsylvania Press titled, *Agents of Opportunity: Sports Agents and Corruption in Collegiate Athletics.*

Table of Contents

Introduction

I once heard O.J. Simpson tell a reporter that after retiring from professional football it wasn't the game he missed so much, but the people involved in it. He said something to the effect of the locker room being the only place on earth where a grown person could continue to be a child, to be immersed in a lifetime joy and get paid for it.

I think this is the primary reason why so many of us ex-athletes endeavor to remain involved in the game long after our playing days are over. Somehow it is more fun to record hours for litigation involving the local university's athletic department than to do the same for a faceless Fortune 500 corporation.

I have been involved in sports all of my life. Like many others interested in this area of law, I am a former athlete who now happens to be an attorney. Friends joke that if I had gone to medical school, I would probably now be calling myself a "sports doctor," and trying to explain the distinctions between myself and any other medical practitioners who work with athletes. Currently, I practice and teach sports law. I also write about problems in athletics and I am married to a former professional tennis player. So why not a book on careers in sports law?

This monograph is based primarily on questionnaire responses and a series of interviews conducted with members of the American Bar Association's Forum Committee on Sports. The material presented here should provide students and practitioners interested in sports law with information that will help make academic and career decisions easier.

Although not examined at length here, there are a number of non-legal positions in sports which attorneys frequently fill. The most prestigious of these are league commissioner posts. In recent years attorneys have also organized Olympic games and sports festivals as well as owned and managed individual professional sports franchises.

These non-legal alternatives demonstrate the range of opportunities available to those who choose a career in the sports industry. The interviews that follow offer a look at what a career in sports law is all about.

What is a Sports Lawyer?

'Sports lawyer' is a meaningless term.
General Counsel, Professional
Sports League Player's Union

Some lawyers responding to our questionnaire asserted that "there is no such thing" as sports law or a sports lawyer. Many added that while an attorney may encounter an issue which involves sports, there is very little law that applies solely to sports.

Admittedly, the term "sports lawyer" may be somewhat nondescript. In fact, an attorney who handles sports related matters must necessarily deal with a wide variety of fields.

The most common involvement of lawyers in sports may be as athlete agents, negotiating player contracts for athletes with professional teams. However, as many respondents noted, contract negotiation does not require a law degree. Indeed, one of the first sports agents was a cartoonist and another was a Hollywood producer.

Still, there is more to sports law than negotiating contracts. An attorney can be involved in many areas of professional and amateur sports. It is difficult to name an area of legal specialization that does not, in some way, have an impact on sports.

What, then, is a sports lawyer? He or she may be: an attorney who specializes in a particular sport; the exclusive legal representative of teams, unions, leagues, or even agents; or a litigator who focuses upon sports litigation exclusively. Often the definition of an individual sports lawyer is determined by his or her employer based on the attorney's responsibilities or role within an organization.

In a later section, we will examine in detail a few of the many roles a sports lawyer may play. But the responses generated by our questionnaire indicate that there are those who spend a good portion of their time, if not the majority of it, involved in the legalities of the sports world.

2
Substantive Law

'Sports law' is a compendium of substantive law.
Sports lawyer practicing in the Northwest

Asked what areas of the law they find most applicable, our respondents listed (in order of frequency) antitrust, contracts, labor, torts, criminal, constitutional, real estate, and taxation law. Let's take a look at each of these areas, noting some of the special characteristics of their application to sports. Keep in mind that litigation is possible in any of these substantive areas as well as others.

Antitrust Law

Antitrust law generally seeks to encourage competition and prevent monopolization in commerce. There are both state and federal statutes designed to prevent agreements in restraint of trade. The statute receiving the most attention in sports litigation is Section 1 of the Sherman Act. (Appendix B)

Probably the most unique law applied to sports is the antitrust exemption judicially granted to the sport of baseball. In 1922, in *Federal Baseball v. Philadelphia Baseball Club*, the Supreme Court of the United States held that Major League Baseball is exempt from antitrust scrutiny. Initially the sport was held exempt because it was not considered to be involved in interstate commerce. The court felt that baseball was purely a local matter, not an area to be governed by federal law. But even after the advent of television and after interstate team travel became the rule rather than the exception, the exemption continued—primarily on the legal principle of *stare decisis*, or "let the decision stand." Although challenged during subsequent years, the legal principle survives. *Flood v. Kuhn* was the most recent Supreme Court affirmation of this exemption in 1972. However, all other sports through a series of decisions following the *Federal Baseball* case were held to be specifically subject to the antitrust laws.

There are three other notable sports exemptions to the antitrust laws. They are: a legislative exemption allowing leagues to pool the sale of broadcast rights, the legislative exemption which cleared the way for the American Football League (AFL) and National Football League (NFL) merger in 1966, and the labor exemption for the terms of union management collective bargaining agreements. The last exemption is applicable in other industries as well.

Many scholars now believe that the baseball exemption only applies to issues of free agency and that a court would not now allow Major League Baseball to exercise any predatory practices to prevent the development of a new league. Interestingly, competing leagues have recently challenged the National Football League, National Hockey League, and National Basketball Association. In recent decades only Major League Baseball has remained unchallenged by a rival league, although a number have been contemplated.

Antitrust litigation has occurred in two primary areas of sports. The first and most prevalent litigation involves player free agency. Players have long contended that they should have the right to freely negotiate with all teams in a particular league—that is, to have a free market system. The teams' owners have consistently asserted that such a system would destroy the "competitive balance" of the league and would result in a direct correlation between the richest and most successful team. Thus the various leagues impose restraints that bind athletes to teams and make it costly for a new team to lure an athlete to sign with them. The major sports leagues now have varying degrees of free agency while the unions continue to fight for greater expansion.

The other area where antitrust issues frequently arise is in regard to team owners' relations among themselves and with the respective leagues. This has been quite evident in the area of member franchise relocations. The most celebrated litigation of this type involved the relocation of the former Oakland Raiders to Los Angeles by managing partner, Al Davis. In *Los Angeles Memorial Coliseum Commission v. National Football League*, the Raiders successfully asserted in 1984 that the National Football League improperly applied its relocation rule in blocking the Raiders initial request to relocate. The National Football League's application of its rule regarding relocation was held to be anti-competitive and in violation of the federal antitrust laws.

Appeals of that case and later litigation involving the 1984 relocation to Los Angeles of the former San Diego Clippers, of the National Basketball Association, have clarified the right of a league to bar a unilateral franchise relocation. However, some issues remain unresolved, and the right of a league to prevent a member franchise from relocating is still not clearly defined.

Contract Law

Contract law delineates which agreements made by individuals or entities are enforceable and focuses on the remedies which flow to a party when an enforceable contract is breached.

Contract law plays a crucial role in sports. Today most player contracts have been standardized into a "boiler plate" format. Generally only the extraordinary athlete can have a standard clause changed or an entirely new contract drafted.

Compelling issues arise in contract law whenever an "upstart" league challenges an established league. The United States Football League ("USFL") raised some issues in its attempts to sign NFL players to "futures contracts"—contracts scheduled to begin at the end of the players' NFL contracts.

Many sports lawyers and athletes cite sports as the one area where individuals feel that they should be able to "renegotiate" their contracts before the term of the existing agreement ends. Egos play a major role in sports where there is a degree of notoriety given to the highest paid player in a particular league or in a particular position. The player contract, however, is not the only agreement in sports. Examples of other contracts include: endorsement agreements for athletes, teams, leagues, and coaches; sale contracts for teams; personal appearance agreements; and virtually any agreement that takes place in the operation of a major sports-related business.

The drafter must have a knowledge of the special idiosyncrasies of sports. For example, the individual drafting an endorsement contract for an amateur athlete must be keenly aware of how each clause may affect that athlete's amateur status. Similarly, the negotiator of a player contract for a professional athlete must be aware of the incentive bonus clauses that may be available to that client within the given sport.

Labor Law

Labor law centers on the agreements and relationships between the labor force and management, which in the United States are largely governed by the National Labor Relations Act (NLRA).

All of the athletes in the major professional sports are represented by players' unions. Likewise, unions represent umpires, referees, and other officials. In each of these sports, the respective union is now recognized as the exclusive bargaining unit for that sport's athletes.

There is also a special relationship between unions and the individual player agents who assume traditional negotiation roles within the union. In most industries, the union negotiates the salaries of its members. In sports, the unions negotiate the minimum salaries and the athletes, usually with the assistance or consultation of an agent, negotiate everything above that minimum.

The union still retains the role of the collective bargaining unit for the athletes. In most leagues, collective bargaining issues include not only minimum salaries, but also the terms of the standard player contract, insurance coverage, retirement pensions, and new areas such as drug and AIDS testing.

A growing issue is the role players' unions should play in regulating athlete agents. The players' associations in the NFL, NBA, and Major League Baseball have all initiated player agent certification programs. The role of these certification programs in regulating agents will be discussed in Chapter Seven.

Tort Law

A tort is a private wrong, not including a breach of contract, for which the party injured is entitled to compensation. Tort actions in sports are rare since there is a recognition that the athlete has "assumed the risk" of injury which may occur as a result of the activity in which he or she is involved. Assumption of such risk is a generally recognized defense to a tort action. Tort actions may be brought when something happens outside of the area of consent implied by the athlete's participation in a sport. At issue is whether the activity goes beyond the degree of consent granted by the participating athlete. Examples are: late hits in football and "beanballs" in baseball. Late hits and beanballs may in some circumstances be considered to be intentional or reckless conduct and potentially subject the tortfeasor to liability. Further issues arise when a plaintiff seeks to extend liability to the referee, stadium owner, team owner, or someone else remotely connected to the cause of the injury.

The areas of libel and slander have received some attention in sports litigation as well. The issues have ranged from a newspaper's alleged libel of a college coach and whether he should be viewed as a public figure to whether or not a coach has a right to criticize an umpire.

A final issue is the unauthorized use of an athlete's name or likeness. The attorney can play an important role in maintaining and protecting the value of an athlete's name for product endorsements.

Criminal Law

Criminal activity in sports can encompass many areas. With the large number of drug problems in professional sports, an athlete may require the counsel of a criminal attorney. Athletes have also been prosecuted for alleged involvement in gambling.

Individuals have also brought actions attempting to equate excessive force on the field with criminal activity. Entire teams have been accused of being a "criminal element" in professional sports.

The regulation of athlete agents is another area where there has been an expanded application of criminal law. Criminal prosecutions, including federal-level indictments, have been made against agents who have been accused of using "overzealous" client recruitment practices. These practices have included threats to break the legs of student athletes who do not enter into representation agreements with the agents.

Constitutional Law

Constitutional law encompasses a vast area. Of primary interest in sports are the individual privacy rights derived from the U.S. Constitution. At present there are two major sports related issues in constitutional law: privacy as it relates to drug testing and the commerce clause as it applies to eminent domain actions against relocating franchises.

The privacy issue in drug testing is being reviewed at both the amateur and professional levels. Generally, there are no rights to privacy in the private sector, since only government employees are awarded this protection outright by the constitution against their employers. There is, however, often a right of privacy provided by individual state constitutions which do extend to private employees against their employers. Some suits by athletes have been successful in preventing testing based on these state statutes. Most privacy issues on the professional level are resolved through collective bargaining. The individual player's union may be able to bargain away state-protected privacy rights.

Apart from the antitrust action against the NFL in the Raiders case already noted, there was a separate action brought by the city of Oakland, California, against the franchise. In the 1982 case *City of Oakland v. Oakland Raiders*, the city asserted that it could exercise its police powers and "condemn" the franchise to stay in Oakland and not move to Los Angeles. Essentially, Oakland sought to condemn the Raiders franchise, utilizing eminent domain arguments generally used to condemn homes to make room for highways or parks.

The court held that because the National Football League was involved in interstate commerce, an area which could only be regulated by the federal government, it was beyond the city's power to condemn an NFL franchise. In effect, the commerce clause of the Constitution barred the city from exercising its power of eminent domain over a professional sports franchise. A similar action was brought, without final resolution, by the city of Baltimore to prevent the move of the Colts franchise to Indianapolis.

Real Estate Law

Many practitioners noted in the questionnaire that their work in real estate and tax law served as an entree into sports. Commonly, if an athlete, team, or some other sports entity had a question regarding a real estate transaction, they would contact a real estate attorney. For example, teams require stadium or arena leases. Players or other sports figures purchase homes and make other real estate investments.

Attorneys who deal in this area might have to structure transactions according to the income pattern of the professional athlete. An athlete's career may span only a few years and therefore, an investment requiring payments over thirty years may not be advisable, even though the athlete currently has a high income level.

Tax Law

There is very little about tax law that is unique to sports. However, as with real estate transactions, the earning patterns of the athlete must be considered in making decisions for the athlete and attempting to gauge the tax impact. Quite simply, the tax aspects of any financial transaction may have an impact on the underlying transaction itself.

Player salaries, the decision to buy or sell a franchise, and federal withholding requirements are all elements of tax law. There have been issues recently ranging from the valuation of player contracts in the sale of a franchise to whether the price of an athlete's sneakers is deductible.

Obviously sports issues can arise in other areas of the law. They include divorces, bankruptcy, partnership formation, copyright, international law issues, and property law rights. Many survey respondents advised those who want exposure to clients in sports to focus on general litigation so that they are prepared to handle any issue the athlete, team owner, or any other sports party may require.

3
Representative Positions

Sports Law is a highly competitive field with few job opportunities for beginners.
A partner in a Northeastern firm representing several sports clients

Lawyers involved in the sports world have diverse responsibilities. As noted earlier, the common perception of the sports lawyer is one who represents athletes in contract negotiations and other personal and business affairs. While many sports lawyers do in fact represent athletes, a vast number also work as attorneys for professional sports teams, leagues, player unions, college athletic departments, and other organizations or individuals.

This section is intended to provide a view of sports law through the eyes of the practitioners themselves. While comments were solicited from as wide a range of sports lawyers as possible, this section does not include comments from attorneys in all areas of sports law. Instead, this section aims to provide the budding sports lawyer with a general perspective on this career, a summary of a typical work week of a young sports lawyer who acts as an agent, and the typical week of a general counsel for a major sports management and marketing firm.

Agents

Start with one good client and let word of mouth develop your client list.
Private practitioner, Southern law firm

The first prominent sports agent was not an attorney but a theatrical agent. C.C. Pyle, the agent for the legendary football player Red Grange, reportedly negotiated a contract in 1925 paying Grange $3,000 per game, as well as an additional $300,000 for endorsements and movie rights. The legendary Babe Ruth consulted an agent (reportedly a cartoonist) for financial advice during the stock market crash and a Hollywood movie producer represented superstar pitchers Don Drysdale and Sandy Koufax in a holdout for $1 million.

These stories point out that many sports agents are not lawyers. In fact, the only thing a non-attorney agent cannot do is practice law.

Called athlete representative, athlete agent, sports agent or just "agent," attorneys who are players' agents are probably more frequently in the public eye than any other attorneys. While negotiating an athlete's playing contract is a major function for the player's attorney, these lawyers may take on a number of other duties.

Athletes' attorneys are often involved in managing a client's business and personal needs as well, including the expected: endorsement contracts and personal investment decisions, and the unexpected: divorce or criminal violation.

Several lawyers stated that the biggest obstacle facing an athlete's attorney initially is obtaining clients. There are many "unscrupulous agents who have ripped off athletes in the past, and have given the rest of us a bad name," one attorney noted.

Another suggested that the best way to break into the field is to "grow up next door to a number one draft choice." Humorous as that comment may be, many of the attorneys surveyed did in fact say that having an 'in' with an athlete helps build a name in the business —perhaps someone they met on campus or an athlete from their hometown.

"If you do a good job with that first sports client, you'll get your name around," one practitioner advised. "That's the best way to do it."

The numbers demonstrate how competitive the field is. In 1987, the National Football League Players' Association reported that there were 750 registered agents and only 1,260 active players. In 1986, prior to the imposition of a $200 registration fee, the number of agents exceeded the number of players. In 1987, the National Collegiate Athletic Association reported having 450 agents registered and only 497 athletes that would be drafted by the National Football League and National Basketball Association combined.

While the solo sports attorney is still quite prevalent, a number of attorneys have gained entry into the field by working for sports management companies. These firms not only handle an athlete's legal affairs, but virtually every other aspect of his or her business dealings, public relations activities, promotional work, and tax planning.

In addition to attorneys, sports management firms employ recruiters, accountants, financial planners, tax accountants, and tax attorneys. The setup has a number of advantages over a solo practitioner or an attorney in a traditional large law firm, according to one attorney who works for a sports management company.

"By having all services under one roof, we can coordinate all activities more easily," he said. "For example, if we know a player is at the end of his career, this improved coordination allows us to better prepare the athlete for the future."

A sports management firm often employs non-attorneys as full-time recruiters, thus helping the attorneys avoid the somewhat thorny ethical issue of soliciting new clients. These issues are explored more thoroughly in Chapter Six.

Generally, only the "big-name, high-draft choices" rate large-scale marketing and promotion services, explained one attorney in a sports management company. For most athletes, the firm will be more concerned with more general legal services and the financial well-being of the client. Another attorney noted that while representing an Olympic gold medal-winning boxer, he couldn't find an endorsement opportunity anywhere.

Thus, the terms *athlete representative, sports attorney, athlete agent,* or *account executive* at the larger sports management firms, encompass much more than the glamorous few who make headlines in negotiating multi-million dollar contracts. These attorneys must be proficient in many areas of substantive law, and be prepared to face many legal problems and challenges.

A critical concern of many interviewed was that practitioners recognize their limitations. Sports law, as in any other profession, is not an area where someone should try to be a "jack of all trades." When an athlete hires an attorney to negotiate a contract, there is no obligation to manage the athlete's earnings as well. If the attorney does not have a background in the field, the appropriate route may be to refer the athlete to a skilled money manager.

The same is true in a number of other areas. One attorney noted that when his client was faced with drug charges the best service he could provide was to locate a good criminal attorney.

"If you do a good job for your client on the referral side," he explained, "he'll respect you that much more."

Often the player's attorney acts generally as a coordinator. If the attorney is not part of a full service management firm and does not possess all the skills needed, referral to other lawyers or association with a law firm may be the best alternative.

A Sports Lawyer's Week

Bruce Brown is an attorney who has worn the sports lawyer label since 1985. He kept a log of his sports related activities during a recent week to produce the following inside look at his sports practice.

Monday: I had a breakfast meeting with a professional football player to discuss upcoming personal appearances for him individually, and as a member of his team's defensive unit. We discussed the pros and cons of each proposal, in addition to the payment for each, and whether he would retain the payment or donate some portion of it to his favorite charities.

Upon returning to my office, I had a conference call with a professional baseball player and an accountant for his foundation. We are planning a fund-raising golf tournament for next May and we needed to ascertain if all entry fees, etc. will fall within the 501(c)(3) exemption of the I.R.S. Code.

The afternoon was spent sending out promotional material regarding my management and marketing firm, Renaissance Sports Management, Inc., to 20 college football players whom I am recruiting for representation.

Tuesday: The entire day was spent in Landover, Maryland, where I was negotiating an "offer sheet" for a professional basketball player. We finally finished the session at about 6 p.m.

Wednesday: The first two hours of my day were spent with an artist whom Renaissance Sports contracted to prepare portraits of various sports figures.

The remainder of my day was spent speaking with parents of prospective football clients regarding aspects of my sports practice.

Thursday: I spent the morning at a meeting for potential investors in the acquisition of a network's television affiliates. I was there on behalf of three of my clients, who are forming a corporation to invest in this acquisition. This afternoon I met with a professional basketball player to discuss the endorsement deal that was negotiated yesterday.

Friday: Today I met with a potential client to discuss the prospects of my representing him in his endorsement deals.

View from a Sports Marketing Firm

Pam Lester, a member of the firm Akin, Gump, Strauss, Hauert Feld in Washington, D.C., was the former general counsel for Advantage International, a full service sports marketing firm. While with Advantage she recorded the following highlights of a typical week.

Monday: I proofed 16 contracts drafted by the Legal Department paralegal. These contracts included player endorsements, tennis exhibitions, player commitments, Advantage representation agreements, and various other agreements.

Numerous exchanges of correspondence and meetings continued regarding a swap of office space held under an option by Advantage with a law firm on our floor. This has involved daily negotiations with representatives of the law firm and the management of the building.

Tuesday: Meetings were held and correspondence was sent regarding the termination of an Advantage employee.

Numerous telephone conversations, correspondence, and conferences took place regarding problem investments made by the former agent of a current Advantage client. Investments seemed to have been made negligently, without the client's consent, and with undisclosed commissions payable to the former agent. Most discussions centered upon the chances of recovering in a suit against the former agent, and minimizing the losses on the various investments.

I conducted research regarding Virginia general partnership law for investment partnerships. I also located an attorney willing and able to assist a Swedish client in obtaining a green card.

Wednesday: I conducted settlement discussions regarding the early termination of a client's endorsement contract arising out of the client's appearance in a competitive product advertisement. In this case, it appears that the client's appearance in the other advertisement was beyond his control, and settlement discussions center upon the third party assuming liability for early termination.

I advised our Connecticut office regarding the breach by a third party of a sponsorship agreement for a tennis exhibition.

I wrote our Japanese counsel regarding the possibility of trademarking the name "Advantage International" in Japan.

Thursday: I prepared an in-house memorandum regarding the consequences of Advantage being deemed a government contractor or subcontractor based upon possible contractual relationships with government entities or contractors.

I also conducted research regarding the necessity of athletes joining various actor unions in order to appear in television commercials when those athletes are not primarily engaged in the profession of acting.

Friday: I wrote a letter to competitors putting them on notice that an athlete with whom they were speaking was under contract to Advantage.

I held negotiations and made revisions to several endorsement contracts previously drafted and delivered to the other party.

The final part of the day was spent drafting and negotiating non-monetary terms and re-drafting a major NBA contract.

While there is no such thing as a typical sports lawyer, these logs illustrate some of the excitement of sports law and how it is often balanced by what some consider standard, mundane legal work. Keep in mind that the typical week of an attorney who chose another field could include hours of research in a law library and drafting pleadings for litigation, not just the glamour of trying a case in court.

Anyone pursuing the athlete agent business should also consider the athlete's perception of the agent's role. An article written by former NBA player and Harvard Law School graduate Len Elmore discussing this issue is included in Appendix D.

Players' Union Attorneys

*The focus of bargaining in the team sports
has shifted to union-management and away
from individual bargaining.*
General Counsel, professional sports league players' union

The primary task of the union attorney is to negotiate his or her union's collective bargaining agreement with league management. Once the bargaining agreement takes effect, the union lawyer's job is to file and handle grievances for players based on alleged violations of the agreement. The attorney also has the ongoing task of correctly posturing the union for the negotiation of the next collective bargaining agreement.

The grievance process can be very time consuming.

"If a player does have a grievance, you're involved with that player pretty heavily," said one players' association attorney. "The entire process takes an average of six months to a year."

To avoid such a lengthy proceeding, a team attorney, or even a coach, may call the union attorney asking for an interpretation of the collective bargaining agreement which could possibly head off a grievance.

Aside from work on grievances, the union attorney spends much of his or her time, according to a respondent, "on the phone answering questions from agents about the interpretation of various contractual provisions." As was noted in Chapter Two, sports unions have a unique relationship with agents. The traditional role of a union is to negotiate key terms of employment for its members. That is true in sports as well. However, one important term is negotiated by the agent—salary. Recently the NFL, NBA, and Major League Baseball players' associations have held a tighter reign on agents. The agents must be certified by the union before they may negotiate a player contract.

Much of the attorney's time in these offices is spent consulting with and advising player agents. They are becoming more actively involved in certifying and decertifying agents as well in efforts to regulate the industry.

One union attorney noted that a lot of his work is quite basic.

"For example, if a player is traded," he explained, "we give him information as to his entitlement for moving expenses."

Unions in sports are confronted with many of the same issues that other unions in this country must deal with. Sometimes an issue, such as drug testing, takes on an even greater magnitude due to the unique position of sports in society.

Teams

As a team lawyer, my experience is not much different from that of any other corporate lawyer.
General Counsel, Pro Football Franchise

A professional team is an ongoing business, so the attorney must handle a number of different legal problems.

"When you represent a team, you're representing it as general counsel," one team attorney noted. "The things you get involved in go beyond sports per se."

Whether a team will have full time in-house counsel varies from franchise to franchise. Even if a team does have in-house counsel, the team probably retains an outside firm as well, particularly for time-consuming litigation matters.

Contrary to the general perception, team lawyers are not exclusively involved in the negotiation of player contracts. That task is often left instead to individuals at varying management levels in the front office or possibly even outside counsel. One team attorney said that "from a legal standpoint, player contracts are possibly the least legal-intensive of all your activities." In fact, often the only term negotiated in a standard player contract is the player's salary.

Instead, the majority of the team attorney's time is spent on other duties. The attorney will, according to one practitioner, "deal with tax considerations, management operations, office leases, monitoring litigation—all of which arise in any business."

Some team attorneys often act as the spokesperson for the team explaining various team actions such as why a franchise has relocated or why a star player is not being signed. In contrast, other teams keep the attorney in the background and use that person's legal skills as a traditional business would.

Individual Sports

If you ever shake hands with any of the major boxing promoters, count your fingers afterward.
Attorney/Boxing Manager

Sports such as golf, tennis, boxing, and a number of other individual or non-team sports often require an attorney with a unique knowledge of those industries. Often, particularly with a sport such as boxing, the attorney is the only representative the athlete has. This is true because many sports are not unionized.

These non-team sports often require the athlete to enter into some type of contract for each event he or she participates in. Depending on the athlete's ability, there may be a great deal of flexibility in the negotiation of each contract. In order to obtain the best possible deal, the negotiator must know the market.

In golf and tennis, most athletes are represented by one of the major sports management firms. By virtue of their reputation of having a large number of clients, as well as their managing of events, sports management firms generally have an awareness of the terms that should be included in an athlete's contract.

Boxers are generally represented by individual attorneys or traditional law firms. One attorney noted that the key in that industry is to "know what the network is paying the promoter for the show."

Lawyers who represent individual sport athletes often share the limelight with their client. There was a great deal of publicity regarding the role of attorneys in the life of heavyweight boxing champion Mike Tyson. They were involved in the litigation and settlement regarding the boxer's management contract and in his personal life.

Amateur Athletics

Amateur sports, particularly collegiate athletics, is an area where there is growth potential.
Head of Sports Department, Northeastern law firm

The primary concern of an amateur athlete is insuring that his or her amateur status is not jeopardized. There are several delicate issues involved in protecting an athlete's amateur eligibility. An attorney may be contacted by an amateur athlete to address issues of eligibility, appearance monies, rights regarding drug testing, making a charitable appearance, or other areas. The limitations of what an athlete may do and still maintain his or her amateur status are set forth in the rules of each sport's governing body.

Before taking on an amateur athlete as a client, the attorney must be completely clear on what role the respective amateur rules allow an attorney to play. For example, the National Collegiate Athletic Association (NCAA) does not allow an athlete to sign with an agent before that athlete's class graduates. However, the attorney may be able to advise the college athlete regarding other matters.

If the client is a college athlete, the appropriate governing body should be consulted. In non-collegiate sports there are often national, as well as international, governing bodies which have rules regarding amateur eligibility. Often these governing bodies publish their rules.

Another career possibility is working as an attorney for one of these governing bodies. Lawyers for these organizations must have a working knowledge of the Federal Amateur Sports Act, as well as all national and international regulations.

The attorney who is excited by college or other amateur sports should consider pursing an interest in this growing field.

Arbitration

Arbitration has played a significant role in resolving issues in the professional sports industry.
Partner, Eastern law firm

Arbitration is a means of resolving disputes as an alternative to litigation. In sports the agreement to arbitrate usually is placed in the contract between potentially adverse parties. By doing so, they agree in advance that any dispute between them will go to an arbitrator instead of a court.

Many of the major legal decisions in sports were made, not in court, but in an arbitrator's office. The so-called emancipation proclamation for baseball players came in the 1975 arbitration of Andy Messersmath and Dave McNally. Now salary disputes are frequently resolved this way and many collective bargaining agreements stipulate that disputes between players and their team or league will be resolved through the arbitration process.

The attorney may play a variety of roles in this process. For example, an attorney representing an athlete in other matters may be retained to represent the athlete in the arbitration. The attorney representing the athlete in an arbitration proceeding may also be a union attorney. Obviously, on the other side of the table there will be an attorney from the league office or a representative from their outside counsel.

Attorneys also serve as arbitrators, a neutral person selected by a pre-determined process to hear both sides. The person chosen to be arbitrator may be a law professor, practicing sports attorney, or someone from another field.

Leagues

There is truly something new every day.
Attorney, Professional Sports League

In most instances, the league office is the office of the commissioner or president of that league. Leagues and teams either have in-house counsel or utilize outside counsel. Often, the general counsel for a league will utilize outside counsel for litigation or consultation on non-routine matters.

League attorneys have entered an interesting era in sport. With recent franchise relocations, a good deal of focus is placed on league franchise agreements and individual franchise relationships to other franchises as well as to the league itself. One argument that leagues have tried unsuccessfully to have supported judicially, is recognition of a league as a "single entity."

This single entity designation would exempt a league from antitrust scrutiny. With little success, leagues are now arguing more vigorously against the fiduciary relationship teams have to each other.

In summary, while one focus of the league attorney is on the relationship of the teams to each other, the types of actions that these attorneys have supervised, apart from franchise relocation actions, have included: antitrust actions regarding free agency, the draft, and the right to obtain a franchise; individual rights in drug testing; and trademark actions regarding the rights to utilize the league name and logo in marketing.

As this chapter indicates, the many roles attorneys can assume in the sports world are almost as varied as those taken on by the clients they represent.

Work Settings and L   of Sports Practi.

My office is wherever the ath.   ure.
West Coast athlete agent who practices out of his home

Sports attorneys practice in a variety of settings. The atmosphere ranges from a luxurious office in a large Wall Street law firm to the small, sparsely-decorated office or apartment of the new solo practitioner. In between these extremes are those working at league or team offices or in one of a growing number of full service sports management firms. The lifestyles of sports attorneys and the physical appearance of their offices may be as different as the types of services they provide.

Location and Travel

Sports attorneys are located in all kinds of places, but seem to reside primarily in urban settings. Many professional sports teams and universities utilize attorneys and law firms located in their respective cities.

The amount of travel the individual attorney does depends upon the type of practice. Anyone who desires to represent athletes must spend a lot of time on college campuses recruiting clients. One attorney noted that constant contact with prospective clients is the most important element in signing and keeping those clients.

Many agents spend the appropriate season on the road following their clients. Often this presence makes the difference in the athlete's decision to sign with an agent.

On occasion, team representatives find themselves traveling to the relevant league offices, most of which are located in New York City. The reasons for their visits range from general meetings to representing their clients at a league draft of amateur talent.

And, of course, an attorney may be required to travel wherever there is a sporting event involving his or her client or other athletes.

Lifestyle

The lifestyle of the sports lawyer will depend largely upon the location of the practice, the types of clients, the attorney's success, and his or her personal preferences.

Some attorneys as well as non-attorney agents create an image that they feel will enhance their business. The perception that the young athlete would be more receptive to the overtures of the owner of a Rolls Royce as opposed to the driver of a Toyota is not totally false. But the most significant factor for athletes deciding whether to retain an attorney should be the lawyer's ability, not any superficial gimics.

In the questionnaire many attorneys acting as agents lamented that constant time on the road strained their personal lives, although the effects of such a fast-paced life vary from individual to individual.

Despite a lawyer's successful achievements, he or she can fall prey to temptation. The personal lives of some attorneys in the field have been tainted by an association with prostitutes and drugs, allegedly used to recruit clients.

Compensation

The compensation of the sports lawyer depends on the type of practice he or she pursues. Understandably vague in their answers to this question, most respondents emphasized that the salary could fall anywhere within a wide range.

Payment for the sports lawyer acting as an agent, for example, will vary according to the number of clients. Obviously, the more clients, the more the individual is likely to earn. The rate that the attorney charges is also a factor. The most common method in determining the fees is to charge a percentage of the income the athlete is to receive from the contract the lawyer negotiates. Another alternative is for the attorney to be compensated on a traditional hourly basis. Players' associations, in their certification programs, are now setting ceilings on how much an agent can charge an athlete for contract negotiations.

Attorneys at law firms will receive salaries comparable to others in their graduated law school class at similar size firms. Traditional legal services firms generally bill their clients on an hourly basis, although certain law firms representing athletes in negotiations charge athletes a percentage of the negotiated contract. Attorneys who represent a more traditional client, such as the owner of a franchise or a particular sporting event, are likely to bill at a traditional hourly rate.

Women and Minorities in Sports Law

It is frightening that there are major sports marketing firms with hundreds of employees and not a single black attorney.
West Coast sports lawyer

We're just dealing with a situation in sports where most managers and owners are white and male, and that has its inherent barriers to women and minorities.
Minority attorney, Eastern law firm

Although women and minorities have been underrepresented in this industry for some time, the general issue was brought to public attention by the now infamous statements of former Los Angeles Dodgers Vice President Al Campanis and former CBS broadcaster Jimmy "the Greek" Snyder.

Al Campanis's statement that blacks lacked the "necessities" to hold management positions in sports was probably most indicative of a long-held establishment attitude in sports. While sports law is an exceedingly difficult area for anyone to enter, women and minorities may have an even tougher time breaking into what has traditionally been an all-male, all-white domain. Over the years sports has been recognized as a sector of society with tremendous problems in minority employment, particularly at the management level.

Women and minority sports lawyers are said to encounter many barriers. First, there is a recognized shortage of minority and women attorneys in general, particularly at the major law firms or sports management firms that tend to represent sports clients. Second, the number of minorities and women involved in the sports industry is small, the highest percentage being the athletes themselves.

As with the general management outlook in sports, the prospects for increased participation of minorities and women in sports law is looking brighter, but is by no means rosy. Today, one black sports attorney estimated, there are only a half-dozen full time black sports lawyers in the United States and probably similar figures of other minorities and women. There has been no accurate count taken, and the nature of this field would make such a tally difficult. However, it is clear that the numbers are negligible.

"There are obvious obstacles minorities face in general, but they are really no different than in any aspect of life," the same attorney said. "For example, a lot of general managers had never dealt with a minority or female professional in negotiation sessions. That was something they had to get over."

A female sports attorney said that being a woman or minority was not so much of a disadvantage towards entering the field, but rather that, "There are just very few opportunities for anyone trying to enter the field in general."

As a woman though, her biggest problem was with management. "Their expectation was that to be involved with professional sports, you need a background in the game," she explained. "But as an attorney, I could do my job just terrifically without having to recite statistics."

Since such a large percentage of professional athletes are minorities and a significant portion are women, one might think these numbers would work to the advantage of a minority sports lawyer. One black attorney interviewed agreed with this assertion.

"If you are competent and you are good, we should be at the point where black athletes or female athletes will put their faith in a black or female lawyer," he said. "But it can also work against you, as some black athletes still hesitate to deal with a black in a professional role, or a female athlete (and even a male athlete) will hesitate to deal with a female lawyer in a professional role. It's the old stereotypes at play."

Women and minority attorneys can get into the sports industry in several ways. One minority attorney had been involved in sports all of his life, including a college football career. His entrance into the field of sports law was not planned but "just sort of evolved." After law school, he worked in a law firm where a friend introduced him to a professional football player. First he did some business work for this athlete, then represented him in contract negotiations. Word got around, and before long, 90 percent of his practice was sports law.

As for his advice to minorities and women hoping to enter the field, this attorney warned that the would-be sports lawyer, "must be prepared for a tough, tough battle.

"It's extremely hard to break in," he admitted. "And once you break in its even harder to stay in.

"In this business you have non-lawyer agents involved, and some really have no ethics," the lawyer lamented. "You have just got to work very hard at it."

Of the female sports attorneys interviewed, one arrived by design and another by accident. The first woman said that she had "a lifelong involvement in sports which naturally led to an interest in sports law."

The second respondent ended up in sports law coincidentally. Oddly enough, while she was a practitioner in a law firm which represented a number of sports clients, she never worked with any of them. But when one of the firm's partners became commissioner of a professional sports league, she was asked to come along as the league's general counsel. She took the job, she said, "much to my brother's chagrin and amazement."

While both women encourage other women to enter the field, both emphasize the roadblocks faced by anyone trying to become a sports attorney. As one of the women said, "I think my advice for a woman hoping to enter the field would not be any different than my advice to a man: Learn as much as you can, show yourself to be a hard worker who can wipe the stars out of his or her eyes, and get the job done."

6
Ethical Considerations

*It seems very difficult to develop a
clientele if you are honest.*
Partner, Southern law firm

There are a few unique ethical considerations that pervade the
sports law field. As has been noted, this is a highly competitive field
and it's not always easy to obtain clients. Because of this, and the
competition with non-attorney agents, there may be a greater temptation than in other areas to step outside of the long established legal
profession's Canon of Ethics. Ethical issues, along with criminal prosecutions, probably receive the greatest amount of coverage by the
press.

Solicitation

Non-attorneys may directly contact a student athlete and request
to serve as his or her representative. Attorneys may not do so. In
theory, the attorney may obtain clients only by referral. In an area
of the law known for cut-throat competition, how can one obtain
clients without soliciting, particularly when one does not have a
reputation as a high powered sports attorney?

What in fact happens is that many attorneys do solicit. Not all
attorneys solicit and not all solicit to the same degree, but it does
occur. Obviously, they hope to avoid detection and sanctions by the
appropriate bar association.

Other attorneys establish a separate entity, apart from their legal
practice, through which they can contact athletes without ethical
scrutiny. For example, as opposed to presenting himself as "Joe Zilch,
attorney at law," the individual may establish a management firm and
use the business description of "Joe Zilch and Associates." In theory,
there should then be no scrutiny by the legal community because
Joe's solicitation is no longer being made in his capacity as an attorney.

Apart from solicitation, there is the problem of overly zealous
recruitment of student athletes. Some of these tactics include the

use of money, prostitutes, and drugs to influence athletes to sign with an athlete agent. It is these types of activities that have prompted many state legislatures to pass laws to control recruitment activities (See Chapter Seven).

Conflict of Interest

Another ethical problem cited by sports lawyers is conflict of interest. This legal concept recognizes the difficulty that one necessarily has in representing the interests of two separate entities against each other.

One prominent West Coast attorney pointed out that it is up to the individual attorney whether or not to assume the "hired gun" role. He suggested that an attorney could serve as general counsel for one team and represent other teams in the same league in isolated matters.

This problem presents itself in sports, according to one respondent, because there are so few practitioners with experience in a number of sports related issues. With a shortage of experienced sports attorneys to choose from, many teams, leagues, and individual athletes turn to the same attorney or law firm for counsel.

Another area where potential conflicts occur regularly is with the head of a players' association representing individual athletes in contract negotiations. This had been the case in both professional hockey and basketball, where the head of the players' union represented individual athletes in addition to performing his duties as union chief.

The debatable issue is whether an individual can serve the best interest of all athletes in a sport and at the same time look out for the interest of an individual athlete. For example, if the head of a union represents primarily veteran athletes will he or she have a special interest in protecting the interest of veterans over those just entering the league? A more complex issue may be whether the head of a player's union could properly make a decision regarding his or her own decertification or that of a competing agent.

This potential for conflict points to a need for more qualified attorneys practicing in the sports field. The more qualified attorneys there are, the less likelihood of a conflict of interest.

7
Regulation

Frequently, a sports attorney need not do anything other than pass the bar exam of the state in which he or she intends to practice. However for those who want to act as an athlete agent, there may be some additional requirements mandated by the individual states and the appropriate players' union. There was also a voluntary registration program run by the NCAA. This program was terminated due to its ineffectiveness.

Legal commentators and lawmakers have suggested a national independent agency to regulate agents. Others have suggested that the field of athlete representation simply be opened up, and that a free market system will take care of itself. Below is an overview of the registration, licensing, and certification programs currently in place. Anyone desiring to represent athletes should contact the national and local certifying agencies to find information on the most current registration requirement.

States

Dozens of states now require that all persons acting as athlete agents register with a designated state agency. Registration generally requires the filing of an application and the posting of a bond in a legislated amount.

For the licensed attorney, the legislation as it has been written in some states presents a special problem. It is not always clear whether members of state bars are required to register. The confusing language in such statutes often exempt attorneys from registration when they are "acting in the capacity of an attorney." The question, which has not been fully answered, is whether the negotiation of a contract constitutes acting in the capacity of an attorney.

These state statutes have continued to pose problems within the athlete agent field. In 1981, California was the only state with a specific athlete agent registration statute. Ten years later two dozen states had them.

Commentators have been critical of many of the registration statutes. Although most statutes have been adopted to clean up the athlete agent industry, few establish any minimum qualification standards. In fact, the procedure is much like obtaining a fishing license. Although the forms inquire about an applicant's qualifications, registration rarely is denied.

Similarly, there does not appear to be a high success rate in registering individuals. California, a state known for its large athlete population, and one which has had its statute in place the longest, reported only seventeen registrants at the beginning of 1988.

One way these statutes may prove most successful, once agents register, is in prosecuting agents for overly zealous recruiting activities that are not illegal under any other existing laws. For example, paying an athlete money to induce him or her to sign a representation agreement is not generally illegal. However, it would be under many of the growing number of state statutes, and made subject to state, civil, or even criminal sanctions.

Two other general problems have been raised regarding these laws: the commerce clause of the U.S. Constitution and conflict of laws problems. The commerce clause issue concerns the right of individual states to regulate interstate commerce. Athlete agents and the athletes they represent are part of the sports industry which is a national enterprise. The commerce clause prohibits state regulation that burdens interstate commerce, and some commentators believe that these state statutes violate the clause.

Similarly, the conflict of laws issue is concerned with which state law is applicable to an athlete agent in a given situation. For example, if an Ohio-based agent signs an athlete playing for a school in Georgia who is drafted by a team in California, is the agent required to register under all of these states' laws? If there is a problem, which law controls?

Many point to the commerce clause and conflicts problems as reasons to enact federal legislation governing the registration of all athlete agents. Federal legislation would provide necessary uniformity and clarity.

Excerpts of the statute regulating California agents are included in Appendix C. An Indiana statute which requires the athlete to notify the state of the forfeiture of his NCAA eligibility is set forth in Appendix G.

Unions

Currently the National Football League Players' Association, National Basketball Association Players' Association, and Major League Baseball Players' Association require that athlete agents be certified before representing athletes in their sport. Generally, registration with these entities requires one to complete an application, attend an annual educational meeting, and pay a fee.

The purpose of registration both by states and by the players' associations is to protect the athlete both from unscrupulous characters and from well-meaning individuals with inadequate ability to negotiate contracts. The unions aid the agents in the negotiation of the contracts. To insure that the individual agents have adequate information, the unions maintain statistical information regarding the progress of individual negotiations. By doing so, they allow the individual registered agents to obtain data regarding how much athletes comparable in ability, draft round, and other characteristics receive. The individual unions conveyed their legal right to negotiate wages for the athlete to the individual athlete or the athlete's agent. The agent, presumably has the same level of information as does the team he or she is negotiating with.

There was initial concern about whether players' associations could assert any authority over the agents for rookie athletes. Until the athletes became members of the league, they were not members of the players' association and thus it was debatable whether their representation needed to be certified. Assertions by the NBA and an arbitration in the NFL now indicate that even the rookie representatives are covered and must be certified.

Another potential problem in this type of certification program is that it may violate antitrust laws. This issue may be tested if an athlete agent is denied certification. If that occurs, then the league teams have to agree not to negotiate player contracts with an uncertified agent. Thus, there are potential antitrust actions against both the players' association and the league teams. The certification and decertification process may serve as a strong tool in regulating the activities of agents.

NCAA

The NCAA sponsored a voluntary agent registration program. This program, with no distinction between attorney and non-attorney agents, gave individuals the opportunity to sign up and comply with the NCAA's guidelines.

The basic requirement for those who registered was that they contact a school's athletic director prior to contacting an athlete enrolled at that institution. The NCAA made a list of registered agents available to athletes of NCAA member institutions.

The NCAA program did not, however, have the force of law behind it since it was purely voluntary. The program gave a stamp of approval to some individuals that may not have been qualified. The program was terminated in 1990 leaving regulation to the states and unions.

Investment Manager Registration

Generally, if an attorney is not managing the athlete's money, he or she is not required to register under the various state statutes or federal securities laws regarding the management of another's money. Problems may arise, however, when the attorney is managing the athlete's earnings.

The problem is magnified when more than one athlete is represented by the agent and the clients' funds are pooled and invested. One must be extremely cautious if this service is provided. This is a potential area of future litigation.

Association of Representatives of Professional Athletes

This organization of agents has established a code of ethics to regulate itself. Like the NCAA, the organization does not have the force of law behind it, and compliance with its code of ethics is voluntary. A copy of its code of ethics is attached as Appendix E.

8

Advice to Students

*There will always be a role for a
lawyer who has expertise.*
West Coast Athlete representative

The most consistent advice offered by practitioners in this field
to students was simply to become the best lawyer you can be. Most
attorneys noted that being a sports lawyer required no special training prior to beginning actual practice. Some noted that the worst
preparation possible would be to focus solely on the "ill-defined body
of [sports] law."

Many respondents recommended that attorneys hone their litigation skills, because that is the one area where an attorney will most
likely encounter a sports client. Most of those queried also agreed
that maintaining an interest in sports was important.

Relevant Courses

The majority of law schools do not have a standard sports law
course in their curricula. Most practitioners interviewed felt that the
absence of such a course would have little bearing on a student's
future career in sports law. In fact, the consensus was for the student
to attain a wide background in other areas of practice.

However, respondents indicated that a course in sports law would
certainly be worthwhile if one is available. A sports law course should
cover a wide range of substantive areas, particularly those discussed
in Chapter Two.

Finally, it is always easier for a student to obtain a position with
a firm or any entity if he or she has excellent grades. To obtain these
excellent grades, it is advisable for a student to take courses in which
he or she has a strong interest.

Entry Level Positions

One need only reflect for a moment on the total number of leagues,
teams and other sports organizations in this country to realize how

small the sports law field is. It has been estimated that there are fewer than 5,000 positions in professional sports in this country.

The total number of athletes who can afford to retain an attorney is also small. This is truly an area where "who you know" may get you into the business.

Many respondents to the questionnaire suggested that academic preparation and luck provide the best entry into the sports law profession. Some individuals suggested non-legal positions as an alternate way of entering the field.

As with a lot of 'desirable areas,' the best way to get involved is through an internship while you're still in school, or through some kind of directed research such as a law review article," according to one staff attorney with a professional sports league.

The student interested in sports law should identify the area of sports that he or she finds most interesting as early as possible. After deciding on what area to pursue, he or she should find out who in the field is doing that type of work.

The *Martindale and Hubbell Legal Directory* will help identify firms that do some work in sports. However, as the specialty is so small, some firms have no specific department which is devoted to sports practice and a firm may not list sports as an area of specialization. The student should talk with practitioners, professors, teams, leagues, and players to discover where the sports attorneys are and with which firms they are affiliated.

Rarely will the student find an employer recruiting at his or her law school specifically for a sports lawyer. The student must identify potential employers. To assist those interested, several sports leagues and other organizations that may offer opportunities for the practice of sports law are listed in Appendix A.

9

Future Considerations

In the near future, it is likely that sports lawyers will be required to specialize. The phenomenon has already begun. Labor lawyers focus on those aspects of labor law, while antitrust lawyers focus on antitrust issues. We will also see more agents concentrating on a particular sport rather than having limited knowledge about all sports.

The solicitation issue must be resolved. Lawyers must be able to compete on the same level as other representatives. If bar associations do not relax their rules, then perhaps the sports leagues and NCAA need to tighten their sanctions on all agents so that attorneys and non-attorneys alike are subject to the same standards.

Remember that representing athletes is only one facet of a career in sports law. An individual looking to assure a future in sports law should create a new area of practice or find an unmet need within the field and fill it.

Examples of newer areas of specialization include: representation of sportscasters, interpretation of NCAA regulations, formation of international leagues, establishment of trusts to maintain athletes' amateur status, and representing athletes in disputes with agents.

The regulations which apply to athlete agents may be overhauled soon. Recent criminal prosecutions make action imperative. Lawyers who serve as sports agents are often viewed as being a part of what some perceive as a monolithic, unscrupulous entity. Unfortunately many athlete agents are unscrupulous. Ultimately, members of the legal profession itself may have to resolve these problems of the athlete agent industry.

Summary
A career in sports law can be exciting and it can be just another legal position. Obtaining a position focusing on the legal aspects of sports can be as challenging as the practice.

Serendipity may be the major controlling force for entry into the field. But having the skills to handle the opportunity that may arise is an aspect firmly within the aspiring sports lawyer's control.

Sports law is a field ripe for growth and open for the individual who is willing to explore and create new opportunities. With the right preparation and attitude, the opportunities are endless.

Appendix A
Sports Organizations

Agent Organizations

American Bar Association Forum Committee on the
Entertainment and Sports Industries
750 North Lake Shore Drive
Chicago, IL 60611
(312) 988-5579

Association of Representatives of Professional
Athletes (ARPA)
10000 Santa Monica Blvd. *Glendale*
Suite 312
Los Angeles, CA 90067
(213) 553-5607   *818 243-2200*

Sports Lawyers Association
5300 South Florida Avenue
Post Office Box 5378
Lakeland, FL 33807
(813) 646-5091

Leagues

Baseball

Major League Baseball
Major League Baseball
Office of the Commissioner

350 Park Avenue
New York, NY 10022
(212) 371-7800

Minor League Baseball
National League of Professional
Baseball Leagues
201 Bayshore Drive, S.E.
St. Petersburg, FL 33701
   or
Post Office Box A
St. Petersburg, FL 33731
(813) 822-6937

Basketball

National Basketball Association
Olympic Tower
645 Fifth Avenue
15th Floor
New York, NY 10022
(212) 826-7000

Football

Canadian Football League
1200 Bay Street
12th Floor
Toronto, Ontario M5R 2A5
(416) 928-1200

National Football League
410 Park Avenue
New York, NY 10022
(212) 758-1500

Hockey

National Hockey League
Sun Life Building

1155 Metcalfe Street
Room 960
Montreal, Canada H3B 2W2
(514) 871-9220

National Hockey League
650 Fifth Avenue
33rd Floor
New York, NY 10019
(212) 398-1100

College Sports Associations

The National Association of Intercollegiate Athletics
1221 Baltimore Avenue
Kansas City, Missouri 64105
(816) 842-5050

The National Collegiate Athletic Association
6201 College Boulevard
Overland Park, KS 66211-2422
(913) 339-1906

Players' Associations (unions)

Baseball

Major League Baseball Players' Association
1775 Broadway, Suite 2401
New York, NY 10019
(212) 333-7510

Basketball

National Basketball Players' Association
15 Columbus Circle
New York, NY 10023
(212) 541-7118

Football

Canadian Football League Players' Association
1686 Alvert Street
Regina, Saskatchewan S4P 256
(306) 525-2158

National Football League Players' Association
2021 L St., N.W.
6th Floor
Washington, D.C. 20036
(202) 463-2200

Golf

LPGA
4675 Sweetwinter Blvd.
Sugar Land, TX 77479
(713) 980-5742

PGA Tour
Sawgrass
Ponte Verda Beach, FL 32082
(904) 285-3700

Hockey

National Hockey League Players' Association
The Thompson Building
65f Queen Street, West
Suite 210
Toronto, Canada M5H 2M5
(416) 868-6574

Soccer

Major Indoor Soccer League Players' Association
2021 L St., N.W.

6th Floor
Washington, D.C. 20036
(202) 463-2200

Sports Management Firms

Advantage International
1025 Thomas Jefferson St., N.W.
Suite 450 East
Washington, DC 20007
(202) 333-3838

International Management Group
One Erieview Plaza
Suite 1300
Cleveland, OH 44114
(216) 522-1200

ProServ
888 17th St., N.W.
Suite 1200
Washington, DC 20006

United States Olympic Committee

1750 E. Boulder Street
Colorado Springs, CO 80909
(719) 632-5551

Women's Sports Foundation

342 Madison Avenue
Suite 728
New York, NY 10173
(212) 972-9170

Sec. 1. Every contract, combination in the form of trust or otherwise, or conspiracy, in restraint of trade or commerce among the several States, or with foreign nations, is hereby declared to be illegal. Every person who shall make any contract or engage in any combination or conspiracy hereby declared to be illegal shall be deemed guilty of a felony and, on conviction thereof, shall be punished by fine not exceeding one million dollars if a corporation, or, if any other person, one hundred thousand dollars, or by imprisonment not exceeding three years, or by both said punishments, in the discretion of the court.

Sec. 2. Every person who shall monopolize, or attempt to monopolize, or combine or conspire with any other person or persons, to monopolize any part of the trade or commerce among the several States, or with foreign nations, shall be deemed guilty of a felony, and, on conviction thereof, shall be punished by fine not exceeding on million dollars if a corporation, or, if any other person, one hundred thousand dollars, or by imprisonment not exceeding three years, or by both said punishments, in the discretion of the court.

Appendix C
Relevant Sections of California Labor Code

The following are selected sections of California Labor Code 1500 et. seq. regulating athlete agents.

§ 1500. Definitions

The following definitions shall govern the construction of this chapter:

(a) "Person" means any individual, company, corporation, association, partnership, or their agents or employees.

(b) "Athlete agent" means any person who, as an independent contractor, directly or indirectly, recruits or solicits any person to enter into any agent contract or professional sport services contract, or for a fee procures, offers, promises, or attempts to obtain employment for any person with a professional sport team or as a professional athlete.

"Athlete agent" does not include any employee or other representative of a professional sport team, and does not include any member of the State Bar of California when acting as legal counsel for any person.

(c) "Agent contract" means any contract or agreement pursuant to which a person authorizes or empowers an athlete agent to negotiate or solicit on behalf of the person with one or more professional sport teams for the employment of the person by one or more professional sport teams, or to negotiate or solicit on behalf of the person for the employment of the person as a professional athlete.

(d) "Professional sport services contract" means any contract or agreement pursuant to which a person is employed or agrees to render services as a player on a professional sport team or as a professional athlete.

§ 1510. Necessity of registration

No person shall engage in or carry on the occupation as an athlete agent without first registering with the Labor Commissioner.

§ 1511. Applications; form; contents; affidavits or certificates of completion

A written application for registration shall be made to the Labor Commissioner on the form prescribed by the commissioner, and shall state all of the following:

(a) The name of the applicant and address of the applicant's residence.

(b) The street and number of the building or place where the business of the athlete agent is to be conducted.

(c) The business or occupation engaged in by the applicant for at least two years immediately preceding the date of application.

(d) The application for registration shall be accompanied by affidavits or certificates of completion of any and all formal training or practical experience in any one of the following specific areas: contracts; contract negotiation; complaint resolution; arbitration or civil resolution of contract disputes. The Labor Commissioner, in evaluating the applicant's qualifications, may consider any other relevant training, education, or experience to satisfy this requirement.

§ 1512. Investigation of applicant and business premises

Upon receipt of an application for a registration, the Labor Commissioner may evaluate and investigate the education, training, experience, and character of the applicant, and may examine the premises designated in the application to verify to be the principal place of business in which the applicant proposes to conduct business as an athlete agent.

§ 1513. Refusal to grant registration; notice and hearing

The commissioner, upon proper notice and hearing, may refuse to grant a registration. The proceedings shall be conducted in accordance with Chapter 5 (commencing at Section 11500) of Part 1 of Division 3 of Title 2 of the Government Code, and the commissioner shall have all the power granted therein.

§ 1514. Revocation or suspension of registration; reinstatement

If registration of an athlete agent is revoked or suspended, reinstatement of the registration shall be pursuant to the procedures provided by Section 11522 of the Government Code.

§ 1516. Applications for registration or renewal; statement of financially interested persons

All applications for registration or renewal shall state the names and addresses of all persons, except bona fide employees on stated salaries, financially interested either as partners, associates, or profit sharers, in the operation of the business of the athlete agent.

§ 1517. Filing fees; registration fees; fees for branch offices; change of location of athlete agent's office

(a) A filing fee shall be paid to the Labor Commissioner at the time the application for issuance of an athlete agent registration is filed.

(b) In addition to the filing fee required for application for issuance of an athlete agent registration, every athlete agent shall pay to the Labor Commissioner annually at the time registration is obtained or renewed, a registration fee and a fee for each branch office maintained by the athlete agent in this state.

(c) A filing fee shall also be paid to the Labor Commissioner at the time application for consent to the transfer or assignment of an athlete agent registration is made, but no fee shall be required upon the assignment or transfer of a registration.

The location of an athlete agent's office shall not be changed without the written consent of the Labor Commissioner.

§ 1518. Amount of fees

The Labor Commissioner shall set the fees required by Section 1517 in the amount necessary to generate sufficient revenue to cover the costs of administration and enforcement of this chapter.

§ 1519. Surety bond; deposit; amount; certificate of deposit or savings account in lieu of surety bond

(a) An athlete agent shall also deposit with the Labor Commissioner, prior to the issuance or renewal of a registration, a surety bond in the penal sum of twenty-five thousand dollars ($25,000).

(b) For the purposes of this chapter, a certificate of deposit payable to the Labor Commissioner, or a savings account assigned to the Labor Commissioner, shall be considered equivalent to a surety bond, as provided in Section 995.710 of the Code of Civil Procedure, and shall be acceptable to the Labor Commissioner upon such terms and conditions as he or she may prescribe.

§ 1520.   Surety bond; payment to state; conditions

(a) The surety bonds shall be payable to the people of the state of California, and shall be conditioned that the person applying for the registration will comply with this chapter and will pay all sums due any individual or group of individuals when the person or his or her representative or agent has received such sums, and will pay all damages occasioned to any person by reason of intentional or unintentional misstatement, misrepresentation, fraud , deceit, or any unlawful or negligent acts or commissions or omissions of the registered athlete agent, or his or her representatives or employees, while acting within the scope of

(b) Nothing in this section shall be construed to limit the recovery of damages to the amount of the surety bond, certificate of deposit, or savings account.

§ 1521.   Suspension of registration; failure to file new bond after notice of cancellation by surety

If any registrant fails to file a new bond with the Labor Commissioner within 30 days after notice of cancellation by the surety of the bond required under Section 1519, the registration issued to the principal under the bond is suspended until such time as a new surety bond is filed. An athlete agent whose registration is suspended pursuant to this section shall not carry on business as an athlete agent during the period of the suspension.

§ 1523.   Contents of registration

Each registration shall contain all of the following:

(a) The name of the registrant.

(b) A designation of the city, street, and number of the place in which the registrant is authorized to carry on business as an athlete agent.

(c) The number and date of issuance of the registration.

§ 1527. Revocation or suspension; grounds

The Labor Commissioner may revoke or suspend any registration when any one of the following is shown:

(a) The registrant or his or her representative or employee has violated or failed to comply with any of the provisions of this chapter.

(b) The registrant fails to meet minimum requirements as set by the Labor Commissioner pursuant to subdivision (d) of Section 1511 and Section 1534.

(c) The conditions under which the registration was issued have changed or no longer exist.

§ 1528. Revocation or suspension of registration;
hearing

Before revoking or suspending any registration, the Labor Commissioner shall afford the holder of the registration an opportunity to be heard in person or by counsel. The proceedings shall be conducted in accordance with Chapter 5 (commencing at Section 11500) of Part 1 of Division 3 of Title 2 of the Government Code, and the commissioner shall have all the powers granted therein.

§ 1530. Approval of contract forms; contents

Any and all contracts to be utilized as agent contracts shall be on a form approved by the Labor Commissioner. This approval shall not be withheld as to any proposed form of agent contract unless the proposed form of agent contract is unfair, unjust, and oppressive to the person. Each form of agent contract, except under the conditions specified in Section 1544, shall contain an agreement by the agent to refer any controversy between the person and the agent relating to the terms of the agent contract to the Labor Commissioner for adjustment. There shall be printed on the face of the agent contract in prominent type the following: "This athlete agent is registered with the Labor Commissioner of the State of California. Registration does not imply approval by the Labor Commissioner of the terms and conditions of this contract or the competence of the athlete agent."

§ 1530.5. Contents of contract; notice concerning
amateur status

(a) The contract shall contain in close proximity to the signature of the athlete a notice in at least 10-point type stating that the athlete may jeopardize his or her standing as an amateur athlete by entering into the contract.

(b) This section shall also apply to any contract negotiated by a member of the State Bar of California which would be an agent contract if negotiated by an athlete agent.

§ 1531. Schedule of fees; filing; changes; limitation of fee of athlete agent; disclosure in contract of services and fees

(a) Every person engaged in the occupation as an athlete agent shall file with the Labor Commissioner a schedule of fees to be charged and collected in the conduct of that occupation. Changes in the schedule may be made from time to time, but no change shall become effective until seven days after the date of filing thereof with the Labor Commissioner.

(b) If a professional sport services contract is negotiated, no athlete agent shall collect a fee in any calendar year which exceeds 10 percent of the total compensation, direct or indirect, and no matter from whom received, the athlete is receiving in that calendar year under the contract. However, an athlete agent may require security that his or her future fees will be paid under the agreement with the athlete.

(c) Every agent contract shall describe the types of services to be performed and a schedule of the fees to be charged under the contract. This subdivision shall also apply to any contract negotiated by a member of the State Bar of California which would be an agent contract if negotiated by an athlete agent.

§ 1531.5. Athlete agent receiving a player's salary; establishment of trust fund

A trust fund shall be established when an athlete agent is the recipient of the player's salary. An athlete agent who receives any payment on behalf of the athlete shall immediately deposit same in a trust fund account maintained by the athlete agent or other recognized depository.

§ 1532. Maintenance of records; false entries

Every athlete agent shall keep records approved by the Labor Commissioner, in which shall be entered all of the following:

(a) The name and address of each person employing the athlete agent.

(b) The amount of fee received from such person.

(c) Other information which the Labor Commissioner requires.

No athlete agent, or his or her representatives or employees, shall make any false entry in any such records. All records required by this section shall be kept for a period of seven years.

§ 1535.5. Ownership or financial interest in same sport; prohibition

(a) No athlete agent shall have an ownership or financial interest in any entity which is directly involved in the same sport as a person with whom the athlete agent has entered an agent contract or for whom the athlete agent is attempting to negotiate a professional sports service contract.

(b) This section shall also apply to any member of the State Bar of California when advising athlete clients, when entering contracts which would be an agent contract if negotiated by an athlete agent, and when attempting to negotiate a professional sports service contract for a client.

§ 1535.7. Investment advice; disclosure of any ownership interest

If an athlete agent also advises a client regarding the investment of funds, the athlete agent shall disclose to the client any ownership interest the athlete agent has in any entity regarding which the athlete agent is giving advice to that client.

§ 1539. Division of fees; agreements with university or educational institution employees; participation in athlete agent's revenues by full-time union employees

(a) No athlete agent shall divide fees with a professional sports league or franchise, or its representative or employee.

(b) No athlete agent shall enter into any agreement whereby the athlete agent offers anything of value, including, but not limited to, the rendition of free or reduced price legal services, to any employee of a university or educational institution in return for the referral of any clients by that employee.

(c) No full-time employee of a union or players' association connected with professional sports shall own or participate in any of the revenues of an athlete agent.

(d) This section shall also apply to any member of the State Bar of California.

§ 1540. Repayment of fees and expenses; failure to obtain employment

In the event that an athlete agent collects a fee or expenses from a person for obtaining employment, and the person fails to procure that employment, or the person fails to be paid for that employment, the athlete agent shall, upon demand, repay to the person the fee and expenses so collected. Unless repayment is made within 48 hours after demand therefore, the athlete agent shall pay the person an additional sum equal to the amount of the fee.

§ 1541. Actions against athlete agent; parties; transfer and assignment; jurisdiction

All actions brought in any court against any athlete agent may be brought in the name of the person damaged upon the bond deposited with the state by the athlete agent, and may be transferred and assigned as other claims for damages. The amount of damages claimed by plaintiff, and not the penalty named in the bond, determines the jurisdiction of the court in which the action is brought.

§ 1546. Noncompliance by athlete agent with 1510; effect on contracts

Any agent contract which is negotiated by any athlete agent who has failed to comply with Section 1510 is void and unenforceable.

§ 1547. Violations of chapter; misdemeanor; punishment

Any person, or agent or officer thereof, who violates any provision of this chapter is guilty of a misdemeanor, punishable by a fine of not less than one thousand dollars ($1,000) or imprisonment for a period of not more than 90 days, or both.

Appendix D
The Agent's Role in Professional Sports: An Athlete's Perspective
By Len Elmore

The sports representative, or "agent," plays many roles. He must be best friend, big brother, father figure, financial adviser, coach, and negotiator for his client. An athlete may not always be looking for all of these traits, but most would be lost without some of them.

The need for a good sports representative arises early in an athlete's career. Once the talented athlete steps onto the court or playing field and shows that special level of skill, that winner's quality, he is instantly touted as a "prospect." "Keep it up and you're a shoo-in for a scholarship, or even a pro contract," the hype-masters proclaim.

While gratifying, this ego inflating can cause more harm than good. It can delude the athlete into an exaggerated sense of self-worth. Once the concept of worth enters his mind, it is time for the sound guidance of an agent.

Today's athlete who seeks sound representation rejects the hope. He looks for candor, objective analysis, and a professional approach that will distinguish the agent of his choice from the so-called "agents with contacts" and other self-styled gurus who have infiltrated the professional and college sports scene. He wants the straight shooter, not the fast talker.

The National Collegiate Athletic Association (NCAA) prohibits any athlete from contracting with an agent (before he is eligible). Sign with an agent, colleges warn, and you lose your amateur status.

In spite of this threat of sanctions, many student athletes succumb to agents' enticing temptations. They accept loans, cars, and other inducements in exchange for promises to sign (illegal under NCAA rules, binding nevertheless).

What Athletes Look for When Choosing an Agent

From my own personal experience and discussions with friends and teammates, it is clear that athletes look for the same things in a representative as do non-athlete clients. A person who is willing to be straight with a player will get the most attention. While outlandish praise and ego-inflating hype may win a few flowers, most athletes eventually see right through the fluff and move on. From my own experience, I remember what impressed me most and what turned me off in my first meetings with prospective representatives. I was very impressed by one agent's professionalism. He made me feel worthy of his attention, and he treated me as an equal, not someone to be taken advantage of. This treatment gave me a clear idea of how he would conduct business on my behalf. Unprofessional conduct came in many forms. A most obvious example was an agent trying to sound like a jive-talking kid and providing dates, limousines, and other seductive lures.

Besides the ability to negotiate a lucrative contract, the good sports agent must have the contacts that are vital to an athlete's earning power. Commercial endorsements, shoe contracts, television and movie deals are but a few of the non- sports opportunities the representative must develop and secure for his client.

Financial Planning

A less glamorous aspect of goods sports representation is sound financial planning. This becomes more obvious when you consider the relatively short earning period of the client as an active professional athlete. The most effective way for a representative to impress a potential client is to develop a general financial plan. This plan should be flexible. It should stress discipline but encourage growth. It is helpful to illustrate the plan with a few examples of other clients, whether athletes or non-athletes, who have succeeded under similar financial guidance. This will impress the client that you are serious about your business and have a record of success.

Maintaining a Good Reputation

In addition to serving as a business advisor, the sports representative must take on the role of trusted friend and confidant. When
you're advising a twenty-five-year-old athlete on the proper handling
of a six-figure income, a little hand holding of the big brother variety
may be very helpful. Even though NCAA eligibility guidelines may
eventually raise the economic level of entering student-athletes, today's athletes are commonly not from wealthy backgrounds. Show
sensitivity and understanding of the player's background and ethnic
culture.

Above all, make the client feel important. Treat him as if he's your
only client, not just part of your stable, whether he's making a million
or the minimum. If you treat your client with disrespect your attitude
will quickly impact on your reputation. It will hurt your chances of
attracting new clients. Insensitive behavior may not put off the superstar clients, but the average and marginal players, who make up
the majority, will stay away. In short, keep your reputation intact—
it's the wrapping on the package. If the players don't like the wrapping, they won't buy the package.

Client Contact

Two words are key to successful client contact: caution and professionalism. In theory, the NCAA restricts an athlete's contacts with
representatives. You may not approach veteran professional athletes
who are already under representation. They must come to you first.

In reality, adherence to these rules rarely occurs. Lawyers and non-
lawyers alike make contacts and attempt to sign players as early as
possible, often before they have graduated. However, more and more
athletes are blowing the whistle on this practice, particularly when
less reputable agents are involved. This results in damaged reputa-
tions, loss of prestige, and possible sanctions against the alleged shady
operator. In the professional ranks, the National Basketball Association (NBA) players union has taken steps to regulate representatives
by requiring registration with, and certification by, the union. Failure
to comply leads to stiff sanctions that can effectively bar an agent's
participation in negotiations with a union ballplayer.

Some agents will, on occasion, do anything to corral a new client.
In my own first encounter with an agent, a perceived friend/fan
turned out to be in the business himself. He had been engaged by

the attorney to solicit business from unsuspecting athletes. Obviously, no one had bothered to consult my coach first. Luckily, I felt I was old enough to choose for myself and didn't get burned. This was in 1974. Today there is a lot more money to be made. (And dare I say fewer sophisticated athletes coming out of college.) The risks are greater. Be careful.

Attracting New Clients

The problem for the aspiring sports representative is that the system leads athletes to choose only among the best-known agents. A catch-22 situation arises when the new representative seeks to attract clients but can't point to a successful track record. Even the most talented superstars rarely sign with an unknown agent. Patrick Ewing and Michael Jordan, for example, are represented by one of the largest firms in the industry. Yet I believe as a first-year law student, I could have negotiated their salaries myself and hired out the financial planning.

Don't forget that the client wants someone who knows what he's talking about. You can accomplish this with rigorous preparation. Court your new client with statistical comparisons, analysis of other players, and knowledge of other team's needs around contract time. Then he will believe that you can handle yourself in negotiations.

Many representatives often resort to offering inducements. Early on, an agent comes to realize that many athletes are easily seduced by the lure of quick cash, a car, and new clothes. After all, what athlete in his right mind is going to accept these gifts and not feel obligated to sign a contract? It isn't worth it, though. Athletes mature and will soon see through this tactic for what is really is—a bribe. Thus, inducements will end up backfiring. They will poison a relationship, resulting in a lost client, not to mention a lost investment.

The same principle applies to inducements for a coach. It's easy for a representative to notice a special relationship between the coach and his player. The agent then offers the coach a fee in exchange for "delivery" of the player. No one would be the wiser, right? Wrong. Not only is it fundamentally wrong, but once this type of deal gets in the wind it is hard to stifle. Apparently, some of the biggest firms do this, but in a more sophisticated manner. I strongly feel that this is morally wrong and downright coercive. It encourages the unscrupulous coach to make a habit of selling his players. The real harm occurs when the athletes find out.

Currently, the corruption is rampant. There are kickbacks from general managers to representatives in exchange for lower contract demands. There are payoffs to agents who "deliver" their clients to shoe companies. It's the nature of the business.

Guiding the Young Athlete through the Jungle: The Coach's Role

The coach and the university can help the young athlete steer through this confusing process. The coach can use his position to screen prospective representatives. Through interviews and investigative work, he can weed out the bad apples and make recommendations. Universities, through their advisory boards, campus services, and a network of faculty and alumni can promote high standards among agents. Yet many representatives and players cry "foul" at these efforts. They accuse university members of caring more for themselves than for the athletes and harboring biases that shut out worthy individuals or firms.

It is wise and important for the sports representative to cultivate the coach's support. In situations involving top athletes, this often results in a line of agents reaching out the coach's door. As long as the coach has no self-interest, he should be fair. Remember, the coach, too, will appreciate a substantive presentation rather than flashy and misleading evaluations and talk of inducements.

Parental Role

Parents are starting to demand a more active role in this process, most notably parents who have some background in negotiations. Even my own parents, who were less sophisticated at the time, took an interest not as much in the bottom line as in the character of the prospective representative. The lesson is simple—don't ignore Mom and Dad.

Conclusion

Now, I know that many of these observations have a didactic ring to them. It's not that I'm a policeman or even a moralist. It's just that I've given the better part of my life to sports. I've seen a lot of friends get hurt. I care. Today young athletes have greater access to information than ever before, in the form of seminars for potential professional athletes and advice from former athletes on the pitfalls of poor agent-client relationships. Sadly, few take advantage of these opportunities. Despite agent registration, credential requirements, and other regulatory devices, exploitation, fraud, and mismanagement continue unabated. One need only look at the sorry plight of one of the greatest basketball players of our generation, Kareem Abdul-Jabbar, to recognize that no player, regardless of intelligence, is immune.

The old rationale for unethical conduct, "if I don't do it someone else will," just doesn't wash anymore. Unless this profession takes a stand, the lawyers who participate in the field will lose the privilege. It's only a matter of time before the abuses of sports representation become the next crusade. Fee limitations are already here in some sports. Because the body of practitioners is expanding rapidly, those of you who participate today must protect your livelihood. A change of direction is needed. It is part of the evolutionary process. You either adapt or go extinct.

Len Elmore, a ten year veteran of the NBA, is a graduate of Harvard Law School. This article is excerpted from a speech given at a Boston Bar Association Seminar on Sports and Entertainment Law held on March 24, 1987. The article was edited by Paul J. Litwin and is reprinted with permission from the Boston Bar Journal, *a publication of the Boston Association.*

Appendix E
Association of Representatives of Professional Athletes' (ARPA) Code of Ethics

CANON ONE

"A Representative shall maintain the highest degree of integrity and competence in representing the professional athlete."

Rule 1-101 Representing Clients with Competence & Integrity

(A) A Representative shall not:
   (1) Violate a rule of conduct of this Code,
   (2) Use another to circumvent a rule of this Code,
   (3) Engage in illegal conduct involving a felony or conduct involving moral turpitude,
   (4) Engage in conduct involving dishonesty, fraud, deceit, or misrepresentation,
   (5) Engage in conduct prejudicial to the reasonable conduct of professional athletics,
   (6) Engage in conduct which adversely reflects on his fitness.

Rule 1-102 Information Regarding a Violation of this Code

(A) A Representative possessing information which is unprivileged as a matter of law and not protected by Rule 4- 101 of this Code concerning a violation of Rule 1-1-1 shall report such information to the Committee on Discipline of the Association of Representatives of Professional Athletes immediately.
(B) A Representative shall be available to testify or produce a statement under oath as to the nature, source and details of the information described in Rule 1-102(A).

Rule 1-103 Refusing to accept a Client

(A) A Representative shall refrain from accepting the representation of a professional athlete when
   (1) The Representative does not possess the competence through training by education or experience in a particular area,

(2) The Representative's representation of the athlete will create differing or unresolvable conflict of interest with an existing client or with an existing financial enterprise,

(3) The Representative has differing interests with those of his prospective client.

(B) A Representative must disclose in writing in advance of his representation of a professional athlete the nature and degree of his involvement in any matter in which he is recommending, suggesting or advising that the athlete invest.

Rule 1-104 General

(A) A Representative shall not knowingly give aid to or cooperate in any way with another in conduct which would violate this Code.

(B) A Representative shall act in the best interests of the professional athlete, bearing in mind the high degree of trust and responsibility reposed in him as fiduciary.

(C) A Representative shall become familiar with the Collective Bargaining Agreement, Standard of Uniform Players Contract, Constitution, Bylaws and League Rules or the League and such other relevant documents affecting wages, hours and working conditions of the players in the sport or sports in which he represents professional athletes.

CANON TWO

"A Representative shall be dignified in the conduct of his profession.

Rule 2-101 Representative's Letterhead, Stationery, etc.

(A) A Representative shall not compensate or give anything of value to representatives of the print, video or audio media or other communication media in return for professional publicity.

(B) The professional letterhead, business or calling card, stationery, announcements, office signs of a representative and his firm or organization shall be dignified and may;

(1) list the representative's name, firm or organization name, firm members and their position,

(2) list the address of the firm's office or offices, phone number, telex and other such information as may aid the professional athlete in locating the representative,

(3) indicate his membership in ARPA.

(C) A Representative in the operation of his firm may practice under a trade name, partnership corporation or professional association.

(D) The letterhead of the representative shall indicate the name or names of representatives associated with the firm. If the degree of participation by a representative in the firm is less than that of a partner or manager, the nature of such association shall be indicated on the firm's stationery.

Rule 2-102 A Representative engaged in more than one profession or business

(A) A Representative who is engaged both in representation of professional athletes and simultaneously in another profession or business shall clearly distinguish those business or professions on his letterhead, office sign, professional card and other public communication.

(B) A Representative, who in addition to his traditional role as a representative, offers to provide services as an investment and/ or financial advisor, counselor or director to a professional athlete in any way assert or maintain control and/or management of the financial affairs of a professional athlete, for compensation or not, must be qualified to do so based upon training or experience.

(C) A Representative who assumes the role outlined in Section B of this Rule, shall fully disclose that role in his contract with the professional athlete he represents. Such contract shall provide at least a statement of the services to be provided in connection with investment counseling, the limitations of such services, if any, and the fees to be charged for such services.

(D) A Representative may use or permit the use of, in connection with his name, any earned degree or title.

Rule 2-103 Recommending Employment of the Representative

(A) A Representative shall not compensate in any way or give anything of value or promise to compensate a professional or amateur athlete to recommend or secure the representative's employment in any capacity.

(B) A Representative shall not compensate or give anything of value to any individual as a reward for recommending the representative's employment or for referring an athlete to the representative; except that a representative may pay the customary costs and charges in connection with a Professional Association and with ARPA.

(C) A Representative may receive without the payment of compensation, other than dues, referrals from appropriate referring agencies.

(D) A Representative may employ for compensation, with the consent of his client another representative or other professional to assist him in fulfilling his duties and obligations to a professional athlete he represents.

Rule 2-104 Fees for Service

(A) A Representative shall disclose, in advance of any representation agreement and in writing, the nature of his fees and the services to be performed for the fee.

(B) A Representative shall not enter into an agreement for, charge, or collect an illegal or clearly excessive fee.

(C) A fee is clearly excessive when, after a review of the facts, an individual within the industry of reasonable prudence would be left with the firm conviction that the fee is in excess of a reasonable fee for the work performed.

(D) Among the factors relevant in determining whether a fee is reasonable are:

    (1) The time, labor, expenses involved,

    (2) The degree of expertise required and the level of expertise of the representative,

    (3) The usual and customary charge in the industry for the services performed,

    (4) The impact of the services to be performed on the workload of the representative,

    (5) The relationship between the fee and the length of the athlete's contract.

(E) In determining his fee, the Representative shall consider the relationship between the fee and foreseeable length of the athlete's employment with the athletic team and shall make every reasonable effort not to inflict serious hardship on the athlete.

(F) A Representative may employ one of the following methods in establishing his fee:

    (1) Fixed fee

    (2) Percentage fee

    (3) Contingent fee

(G) A Representative shall never solicit nor accept any compensation for services rendered in connection with the negotiation of a player contract or in connection with any other services to a professional athlete from a professional athletic team, club or club representative either directly or indirectly.

    (1) Prior disclosure of such compensation shall not result in a waiver of the prohibition set forth in 2-104(G).

    (2) The prohibition set forth in 2-104(G) may not be waived by prior agreement or by subsequent contract.

Rule 2-105 Financial Payments

(A) A Representative shall not offer, promise or provide financial payments, support or consideration of any kind to an amateur athlete, his family members, athletic coach, director, school official or school with the intent to influence those persons or organizations into recommending that representative for employment as a professional athlete.

(B) The provisions contained in 2-105(A) may not be waived in advance or by subsequent conduct.

CANON THREE

"A Representative shall maintain management responsibility for his firm."

Rule 3-101 A Representative working with a non-Representative

(A) A Representative shall not share fees with a non-Representative except:

    (1) A Representative may, with the prior consent of the professional athlete he represents, retain the services of another professional or business entity on behalf of the athlete.

    (2) All charges in connection with such work shall be billed to the athlete directly or, at least, must be separately listed on the representative's bill for services.

Rule 3-102 A Representative and the Player Contract

(A) A Representative shall not negotiate or agree to, on behalf of an athlete, any provision in a player contract which directly or indirectly violates or circumvents an operative collective bargaining agreement.

(B) ALL Representatives shall have a written contract with their clients which fully discloses all fees, duties and responsibilities.

Such contract shall fully disclose all matters in which the representative will receive a financial benefit.

(C) Any dispute arising out of a matter other than a dispute over fee shall be resolved by binding arbitration before an impartial arbitration panel set up for the particular sport in accordance with the rules of the American Arbitration Association.

(D) The supervision and administration of the binding arbitration shall be conducted by ARPA.

CANON FOUR

"A Representative shall preserve the confidence of his client."

Rule 4-101 Maintaining the confidences of the client.

(A) A Representative shall not knowingly reveal information of any sort given to him by a client in the course of their professional relationship and which the client reasonably expects to be kept confidential.

(B) A Representative shall not use such confidential information to the direct or indirect disadvantage, harm, or damage of the client.

(C) A Representative shall not use such confidential information for his own advantage unless the client consents in advance after full disclosure by the representative.

Rule 4-102 Confidential information defined

(A) Confidential information refers to information gained in the course of the professional relationship between a representative and a professional athlete which the athlete has requested to be held confidential or which the representative knows or should know would be embarrassing or detrimental to the athlete if released.

Rule 4-103 Representative's Employees

(A) A Representative may reveal:

    (1) Confidential information with the written consent of the client after full disclosure by the representative.

    (2) Confidential information when required by law or directed by a tribunal.

    (3) Confidential information concerning illegal conduct past, present or future on the part of the athlete, except where such information is protected by the attorney/client privilege.

Appendix F
Suggested Reading Materials

Books

Berry, Robert C., William B. Gould and Paul D. Staudohar *Labor Relations in Professional Sports.* Dover, Mass.: Auburn House, 1986.

Berry, Robert C. and Glenn Wong. *Law and Business of the Sports Industries.* Dover, Mass.: Auburn House, 1986.

Edwards, Harry. *The Sociology of Sport.* Homewood, Ill.: The Dorsey Press, 1973.

Garvey, Ed. *The Agent Game-Selling Players Short.* Federation of Professional Athletes, AFL-CIO, 1984.

Harris, David. *The League, The Rise and Decline of the NFL.* New York: Bantam Books, 1986.

Kowett, Don. *The Rich Who Own Sports.* New York: Random House, 1977.

NCAA. *Manual of the National Collegiate Athletic Association.* Mission Kansas: NCAA (published annually).

Reed, Gregory. *The Business of Boxing and Its Secrets.* Washington, D.C.: New National Publishing Co., 1981.

Ruxin, Robert H. *An Athlete's Guide to Agents.* Lexington, Mass.: The Stephen Greene Press, 1989.

Schubert, George W.; Rodney K. Smith and Jesse C. Trentadue *Sports Law.* St. Paul, Minn.: West, 1986.

Sobel, Lionel S. *Professional Sports and the Law.* New York.: Law-Arts Publishers, Inc., 1977 & Supp. 1981.

Trope, Mike. *Necessary Roughness.* Chicago: Contemporary Books, 1987.

Uberstine, Gary, ed. *The Law of Professional and Amateur Sports.* New York: Clark-Boardman Co., Ltd., 1988.

Uberstine, Gary. *Covering All The Bases.* Buffalo: William S. Hein & Co., Inc., 1988.

Wong, Glenn. *Essentials of Amateur Sports Law.* Dover, Mass.: Auburn House, 1988.

Weistart, John C., and Cym H. Lowell, *The Law of Sports.* Charlottesville, Va.: The Michie Company, Inc., 1979 & Supp. 1985.

Periodicals

Entertainment and Sports Lawyer. Chicago: American Bar-Association Forum Committee on the Entertainment and Sports Industries (published quarterly).

Sports Industry News. Camden, Maine: Game Point Publishing (weekly newsletter).

The Sports Lawyer. Lakeland, Florida: Sports Lawyers Association (published quarterly).

Indiana Code 35-46-4

Chapter 4. Failure to Disclose Recruitment.

Sec. 1. As used in this chapter, "agent contract" means a contract or agreement in which a student athlete authorizes a person to negotiate or solicit on behalf of the student athlete with a professional sports team for:

(1) the employment by a professional sports team; or
(2) the employment as a professional athlete.

Sec. 2. As used in this chapter, "professional sports services contract" means a contract or agreement in which a person is employed or agrees to render services as:

(1) a player on a professional sports team; or
(2) a professional athlete.

Sec. 3. As used in this chapter, "student athlete" means a person who is:

(1) enrolled in a course of study in a public or private college or university and
(2) eligible to participate in an intercollegiate sporting event, contest, exhibition, or program for the college or university in which the person is enrolled.

Sec. 4. A person who knowingly or intentionally:

(1) enters into an agent contract or a professional sports services contract with a student athlete; and
(2) no later than ten (10) days before the contract is executed, fails to give written notice to the head of the athletic department

for the college or university in which the student athlete is enrolled as a student that identifies:

(A) the name and business address of each party to the contract;

(B) whether the contract is an agent contract or a professional sports services contract; and

(C) the date that the contract will be executed; commits failure to disclose recruitment, a Class D felony.